EXPLORING COUNTRIES

Morocco

by Walter Simmons

FORT WORTH LIBRARY

BLASTOFF! READERS
5

BELLWETHER MEDIA • MINNEAPOLIS, MN

BLASTOFF! READERS

Note to Librarians, Teachers, and Parents:

Blastoff! Readers are carefully developed by literacy experts and combine standards-based content with developmentally appropriate text.

Level 1 provides the most support through repetition of high-frequency words, light text, predictable sentence patterns, and strong visual support.

Level 2 offers early readers a bit more challenge through varied simple sentences, increased text load, and less repetition of high-frequency words.

Level 3 advances early-fluent readers toward fluency through increased text and concept load, less reliance on visuals, longer sentences, and more literary language.

Level 4 builds reading stamina by providing more text per page, increased use of punctuation, greater variation in sentence patterns, and increasingly challenging vocabulary.

Level 5 encourages children to move from "learning to read" to "reading to learn" by providing even more text, varied writing styles, and less familiar topics.

Whichever book is right for your reader, Blastoff! Readers are the perfect books to build confidence and encourage a love of reading that will last a lifetime!

This edition first published in 2012 by Bellwether Media, Inc.

No part of this publication may be reproduced in whole or in part without written permission of the publisher. For information regarding permission, write to Bellwether Media, Inc., Attention: Permissions Department, 5357 Penn Avenue South, Minneapolis, MN 55419.

Library of Congress Cataloging-in-Publication Data

Simmons, Walter (Walter G.)
  Morocco / by Walter Simmons.
    p. cm. – (Blastoff! readers: Exploring countries)
  Summary: "Developed by literacy experts for students in grades three through seven, this book introduces young readers to the geography and culture of Morocco"–Provided by publisher.
  Includes bibliographical references and index.
  ISBN 978-1-60014-731-9 (hardcover : alk. paper)
  1. Morocco–Juvenile literature. 2. Morocco–Social life and customs–Juvenile literature. I. Title.
  DT305.S54 2012
  964–dc23   2011032702

Printed in the United States of America, North Mankato, MN.

010112   1203

Contents

Where Is Morocco?

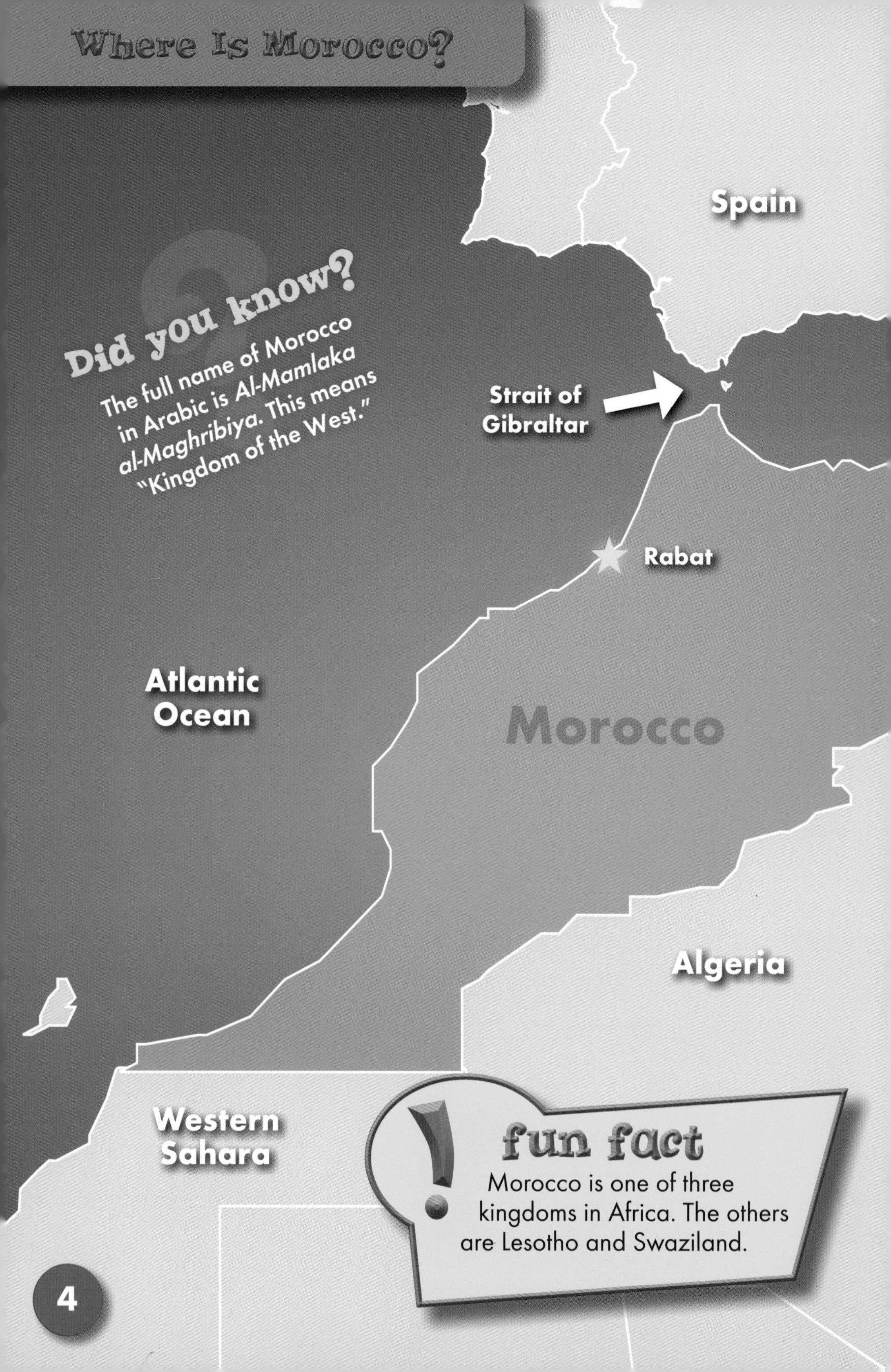

Spain
Strait of Gibraltar
Rabat
Atlantic Ocean
Morocco
Algeria
Western Sahara

Did you know?

The full name of Morocco in Arabic is *Al-Mamlaka al-Maghribiya*. This means "Kingdom of the West."

fun fact

Morocco is one of three kingdoms in Africa. The others are Lesotho and Swaziland.

Mediterranean
Sea

Morocco lies in the northwestern
corner of Africa and covers
172,414 square miles (446,550
square kilometers). Algeria is
Morocco's eastern neighbor.
To the south is Western Sahara,
which Morocco controls.

Rabat, Morocco's capital, lies on
the long western coast facing the
Atlantic Ocean. To the northeast is
the Mediterranean Sea. The **Strait**
of Gibraltar separates the Atlantic
and the Mediterranean. Here the
northern coast of Morocco lies just
8 miles (13 kilometers) from Spain.

N
W   E
S

Rif Mountains

Morocco is a land of mountains, plains, and deserts. The Atlas Mountains begin in southern Morocco. This range stretches across the border into Algeria. The **limestone** peaks of the Rif Mountains rise in northern Morocco. **Fertile** lowlands separate the Rif Mountains from the Mediterranean Sea.

The Sahara Desert covers eastern and southern Morocco. The desert continues across the northern half of Africa. Few people live or work in the Sahara, which gets very little rainfall. Summer temperatures in the desert often reach 120 degrees Fahrenheit (49 degrees Celsius).

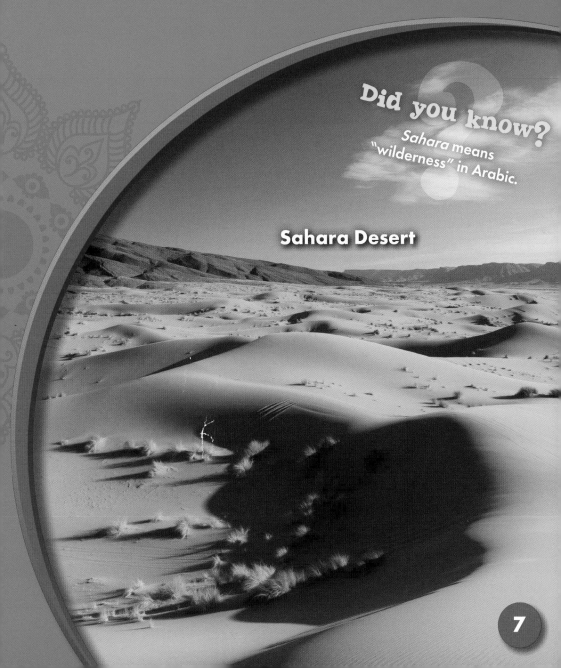

Did you know?
Sahara means "wilderness" in Arabic.

Sahara Desert

Three different ranges make up Morocco's Atlas Mountains. The High Atlas range lies in the center of Morocco. The Anti-Atlas range stretches across the southern half of the country. The Middle Atlas is in the north.

The country's highest point, Mount Toubkal, is in the High Atlas and reaches a height of 13,665 feet (4,165 meters). Forests of oak, cedar, cork, olive, and pine trees grow on the mountain slopes. There is little rain, but snow falls on the mountains in winter.

Middle Atlas Mountains

Did you know?
The Atlas Mountains formed millions of years ago, when the continents of Africa and North America collided. The Appalachian Mountains in the United States form the western half of this ancient range.

fun fact

The leaves and fruit of the argan tree attract Morocco's tree-climbing goats. These animals can easily scamper up and down tree trunks. They balance on slender branches while taking their lunch.

Dry deserts and high mountains in Morocco provide natural **habitats** for many different animals. Mouflon sheep climb high into the mountains. Antelope, deer, and gazelles prefer the plains and mountain valleys.

Did you know?
Barbary lions once roamed Morocco's Atlas Mountains. Though these large, powerful lions are extinct in the wild today, they still serve as a symbol of Morocco.

jerboa

cobra

houbara

In the Sahara, jackals, **jerboas**, and desert hares compete for food and water. Most **species** are active only at night when the temperature is cooler. Many reptiles, including cobras and chameleons, live in cool dens underground. Along the seacoast, marshes provide nesting ground for herons, egrets, ducks, and the houbara, a brown bird that looks like a duck with long legs.

Morocco is home to around 32 million people. The major people groups are **Arabs** and **Berbers**. Most of the people in Morocco follow **Islam** and speak the Arabic **dialect** of Darija. However, French is often used in business and the media.

Arabs and Berbers have lived in Morocco for over 1,000 years. About one out of every three Moroccans speaks a Berber language. Many Berbers live in the Atlas Mountains. Most raise crops or tend herds of sheep and goats. Some Berbers still live as **nomads**, moving from one place to another as the seasons change.

Speak Darija!

Darija is written in script. However, Darija words can be written in English to help you read them out loud.

English	Darija	How to say it
hello	ahlan	AH-lan
good-bye	bislama	bis-LA-ma
yes	eya	AY-ah
no	la	laa
please	'afek	aa-feck
thank you	shukran	SHOOK-ran
friend (male)	saheb	sah-HEEB
friend (female)	sahba	sah-BAH

medina

> ## fun fact
> A *riad* is a traditional Moroccan house. There are no windows facing the street, only a door. The family gathers in a courtyard that has a small garden or a fountain.

The **medina** is a busy place in a Moroccan city. This is the old center of town, where the streets are narrow and crowded. People walk or use motorbikes to get around. In a **souk**, stalls offer food and household goods. Umbrellas or tents shield people from the hot sun. Small workshops offer furniture, carpets, and cookware.

Stone or brick homes are common in the countryside. Older towns are surrounded by stone walls originally built to keep out desert raiders. In the desert, **oases** provide fresh water for villagers and their crops. Some Berber families live in tents made of goatskin. They pack up the tents when they move from place to place.

Where People Live in Morocco

countryside 42%

cities 58%

Did you know?

Morocco was once a colony of France. Many universities in Morocco still teach courses in French.

In Morocco, kids begin school around age 7. Primary school lasts for six years. Students study math, science, and Islam. Some also learn English or French. They then enroll at a *collège*. This is the French word for "middle school." It lasts for three years.

The next step is three years of high school. Students focus on a subject area that will prepare them for university. Some move on to one of Morocco's universities after high school. Others attend technical schools that prepare students for skilled jobs in fields such as computer programming or auto mechanics.

Did you know?

Date palms are one of the world's oldest food plants. In North Africa, people have been growing and eating dates for 5,000 years!

Where People Work in Morocco

manufacturing 20%

farming 45%

services 35%

Moroccan workers make textiles, leather goods, cement, food products, and machinery. The country is one of the world's biggest producers of phosphate. Factory workers process this natural chemical into **fertilizer**. Fishing is also important in Morocco. The catch includes sardines, tuna, anchovies, and shellfish. The country **exports** its seafood all over the world.

Farmers grow fruits, vegetables, olives, and grains. The climate is dry in Morocco, and the country often suffers **drought**. Many farms depend on canals, which bring fresh water from underground **aquifers**. The oases of the desert support the growth of dates, citrus fruits, and livestock.

Did you know?
The tall dunes of Morocco are great for sandboarding. Boarders glide down the tall hills of sand, watching out for snakes and scorpions.

Soccer is the favorite sport in Morocco. Kids play it on grass and dirt fields, or in the streets. Most villages and towns have a soccer field. As many as 67,000 soccer fans often pack into the Mohammed V Stadium in Casablanca. Moroccans also enjoy horse racing and playing polo. In this sport, two teams on horseback compete to drive a wooden ball into the other team's goal.

On the seacoast, people swim, surf, and sail. On the slopes of the Atlas Mountains, several resorts welcome downhill skiers. Many Moroccans also enjoy board games, including **backgammon** and chess. *Zamma* and *kharbaga* are other popular board games. Players move and capture pieces on a square board, much like checkers.

fun fact

Camel racing is popular in Morocco's Sahara region. The biggest camel race in history took place in Western Sahara. The race included 468 Arabian and Bactrian camels.

COUSCOUS

In Morocco, dinner is the big meal of the day. People sit around a low table and take food from bowls with bread or their hands. Many cooks prepare **COUSCOUS** or rice to go with meat and vegetables.

B'stilla is a pastry filled with chicken or pigeon meat, eggs, and almonds. Moroccans also enjoy *Méchoui*, which is lamb roasted on a **spit**. Another Moroccan specialty is *tagine*. This slow-cooked stew features meat, vegetables, and spices.

Moroccans love to drink hot tea flavored with mint. Coffee appears in small cups, often mixed with hot milk. Vendors on the street sell many kinds of juices and *sharbat*. They make this cool drink with milk, ice, and fruit.

tagine

hot tea

Did you know?

Moroccans love spices in their food. Many dishes feature salt, pepper, ginger, and turmeric. Cooks also use cinnamon, cardamom, paprika, saffron, and many others.

moussem of Tan Tan

Most Moroccans celebrate Islamic holidays. Muharram is the first month of the Islamic calendar. People celebrate by opening their doors and offering mint tea, almonds, and dates to visitors. Moroccans also celebrate the birth of the Prophet Muhammad, the founder of Islam. Once a year, many towns hold a local festival called a *moussem*. In the town of Tan Tan, the *moussem* features a camel market and camel races.

Independence Day takes place on November 18. Morocco won its freedom from France on this day in 1956. On July 30, Morocco celebrates Throne Day. This marks the date that King Mohammed VI took power in 1999. The king appears on television to speak to the nation. Parades also take place in cities and towns all over Morocco.

Throne Day

The second-largest city in Morocco is Fez. It is more than 1,200 years old and one of the country's four **imperial cities**. The others are Rabat, Marrakech, and Meknes.

A busy medina lies at the center of Fez. The Blue Gate marks its entrance, and a tall stone wall surrounds it. No cars are allowed inside. More than 9,000 narrow streets form a confusing maze within the walls. Shoppers who navigate the streets are immersed in Moroccan culture. Fez gives them an authentic taste of Morocco.

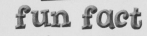

fun fact

Fez is famous for its hats. A "fez" is a tall felt hat in the shape of a cylinder. The hat is red with a tassel on top.

Blue Gate

Fast Facts About Morocco

Morocco's Flag

The flag of Morocco has a red background with a five-pointed star in the middle. The red color stands for the Alaouite Dynasty that rules Morocco. The star is a symbol of the five pillars of Islam. Morocco adopted its national flag in 1915.

Official Name: Kingdom of Morocco

Area: 172,414 square miles (446,550 square kilometers); Morocco is the 58th largest country in the world.

Capital City:	Rabat
Important Cities:	Casablanca, Agadir, Fez, Marrakech, Meknes, Tangier
Population:	31,968,361 (July 2011)
Official Language:	Arabic
National Holiday:	Throne Day (July 30)
Religions:	Muslim (98.7%), Christian (1.1%), Jewish (0.2%)
Major Industries:	farming, fishing, manufacturing, services, tourism
Natural Resources:	phosphate, fish, copper, lead, manganese, salt, iron ore, silver
Manufactured Products:	beverages, clothing, shoes, chemicals, food products, textiles
Farm Products:	olives, dates, citrus fruits, grains, potatoes, tomatoes, sugar, livestock, dairy products
Unit of Money:	Dirham; the Dirham is divided into 100 centimes.

Glossary

aquifers—underground water sources

Arabs—a people group that lives in North Africa and Western Asia

backgammon—a game of skill and chance played with a board, pieces known as checkers, and dice

Berbers—a people group originally from northwestern Africa

couscous—a grain served with many Moroccan meals

dialect—a regional variety of a language

drought—a long period of no rain

exports—sells and sends to another country

fertile—supports growth

fertilizer—a substance that helps plants grow

habitats—the environments in which a plant or animal usually lives

imperial cities—historic cities that were once home to Moroccan rulers

Islam—a religion that follows the teachings of the Prophet Muhammad

jerboas—desert rats that live in burrows and can hop long distances

limestone—a hard stone used in construction; limestone is formed over millions of years from old coral and shells.

medina—the old center of a North African city

nomads—people who have no specific home and travel from place to place

oases—fertile areas in an otherwise dry region; most oases have a spring of water.

souk—a public marketplace in Africa or the Middle East

species—specific kinds of living things; members of a species share the same characteristics.

spit—a rotating grill for cooking food

strait—a narrow stretch of water that connects two larger bodies of water

To Learn More

AT THE LIBRARY
DiPiazza, Francesca. *Morocco in Pictures.*
Minneapolis, Minn.: The Lerner Group
Twenty-First Century Books, 2007.

Merrick, Patrick. *Morocco.* Chanhassen, Minn.:
Child's World, 2000.

Seward, Pat, and Orin Hargraves. *Morocco.*
New York, N.Y.: Marshall Cavendish Benchmark,
2006.

ON THE WEB
Learning more about Morocco
is as easy as 1, 2, 3.

1. Go to www.factsurfer.com.

2. Enter "Morocco" into the search box.

3. Click the "Surf" button and you will see a list of
   related Web sites.

With factsurfer.com, finding more information is just
a click away.

Index